Text copyright © Victoria Searle-Thomson 2024

Photography copyright © Victoria Searle-Thomson 2024

All rights reserved. No part of this work may be reproduced or used in any form or by any means, electronic or mechanical, including scanning, photocopying, recording or by any information storage and retrieval system, without the prior permission of the publisher.

Victoria Searle-Thomson asserts her moral right to be identified as the author of this work.

First published in 2024 by Belsize Books.

NUTS ABOUT...

BAKING

High Protein and Naturally Gluten Free

VICTORIA SEARLE-THOMSON

CONTENTS

Foreword 6

It's not you, it's wheat! 7

Apple and Honey Cake 12

Apple and Raspberry Crumble 15

Baked Vanilla Cheesecake 18

Bara Brith 21

Carrot Cake Pancakes 24

Cherry Bakewell Traybake 27

Chewy Ginger Cookies 29

Crêpes 32

Crunchy Lemon and Poppy Seed Squares 35

Danish Apple Trifle 38

Dark Chocolate Tiffin 42

Granny's Pancakes 44

Hot Cross Buns 47

Lemon and Marzipan Easter Cake 52

Lemony Shortbread Rounds 57

Pear and Frangipane Tart 60

Scones 64

Steamed Treacle Sponge Pudding 67

Sticky Toffee Pudding 70

Squidgy Chocolate Brownies 73

Acknowledgments 76

About the Author 77

FOREWORD

If you've picked up this book because, like me, you're intolerant to wheat, you'll know how difficult it is to avoid as an ingredient. It's in so many products, and a key part of so many recipes.

But, as they say, necessity is the mother of invention. Since I (painfully!) discovered my wheat intolerance a little over twenty years ago, I started working on developing and adapting recipes that circumvented wheat.

I didn't stop there: I've also discovered methods for avoiding the bizarre ingredients that turn up in shop-bought, mass-manufactured (and expensive!) gluten-free foods.

A really exciting avenue is the use of nut flour — which is what I'll be focusing on in this book.

Nut flour is a bit of a superfood. It's not just great as a wheat flour substitute — it's also packed with protein, fibre, vitamins, and brings another dimension to the flavour of your bakes. The sweet nuttiness of almonds and chestnuts complements so many cakes and puddings — as you'll find out over the next twenty recipes.

So, let's get your family favourites back on the menu, and boost the nutrition of those dishes while we're at it.

IT'S NOT YOU, IT'S WHEAT!

I'm often asked, "Why are so many people allergic to wheat these days?" and frequently hear the phrase, "It wasn't like this when I was a child." Well, these people raise very relevant points! There is a reason why many more people have become wheat intolerant in recent years and this epidemic has grown exponentially over the last 40-50 years. It is a relatively modern problem. And it stems from what happened to wheat in the 1970s.

The UK and US governments wanted to help arable farmers - an honourable enough gesture - but they did this by telling the general public that the breakfast they had been eating for generations and had served them very well, was no longer good for them. Instead of eating wholesome, unprocessed, typically protein-based breakfast foods, the governments created a whole new breakfast industry: cereal. They packed these ultra-processed foods full of sugar to help them taste nice and then it was sell, sell, sell!

Fast forward back to today and there is a global obesity epidemic.

Not the breakfast of champions

In 1960, obesity levels in US were at 10%, 12% by 1970 and then jumped to 20% by the mid-80s, after cereal had been introduced, invested in, and heavily marketed as a 'healthy' breakfast. Obesity levels have continued to climb steeply, year on year, and now show that over 40% - that's almost half - of all Americans are obese. Not fat, or dangerously overweight, but obese - a disease that kills.

Australia isn't far behind with levels well over 30%. And the UK is hard on their heels with over 30% of men and women in the UK classified as obese. Even more worrying is that child obesity levels in these countries are already into the teens and climbing. A new generation have now inherited the disease.

(Source: World Obesity Federation, https://data.worldobesity.org)

Hard to digest

Guess what? That's not the only health problem caused by the onslaught of wheat. In order to maximise yields, new strains of wheat were cultivated.

Modern wheat breeding has increased the protein parts in wheat that cause celiac disease, and inadvertently created a high-gluten variant that humans have not evolved to digest. Modern wheat is making us sick.

It is also used in many processed foods as a glue - gluten is sticky. It helps foods stick together or stick flavour to ultra-processed foods.

If you're interested in learning more about how modified wheat has changed, how it has led to the change in eating habits and the growth in a global pandemic of obesity and associated rises in heart disease and type 2 diabetes, online search terms such as "modified wheat 1970", will give the history and explain why we have ended up with the wheat - and related health problems - that we see the world over today.

The World Health Organisation (WHO) and World Obesity Federation provide staggering statistics about how obesity has gathered momentum since the 1970s, in direct correlation to the introduction of modern wheat and the growth of ultra-processed foods.

Frankenfoods in the gluten-free aisle

It can be very hard to avoid this modified wheat that has infiltrated our foods in the last 50 years, unless you read every label as you go round the supermarket. You'll then find that, for many products, your only option is the gluten-free aisle, and on those labels, you'll find another set of horrors!

For example, Xanthan gum, which turns up in many gluten-free products: it is not natural and not a food. It is a man-made additive created by fermenting the carbohydrates from sucralose and fructose with bacteria to produce a sticky substance that then has alcohol added to it, is dried and crushed to a powder. It involves lots of lab time and processing equipment. It's termed an "industrial product" that has been linked to respiratory and digestive issues by altering the gut bacteria. It's also added to toilet cleaner, fungicides and paint. I don't find that information at all appetising! It can also come from wheat sugar so if you're wheat intolerant, you need to know where the sugar source has come from. It's not a given that it's suitable for people with a sensitivity to wheat!

The gluten-free market is littered with ingredients that aren't 'real' foods, and whether you have a serious wheat allergy or just want to reduce your wheat consumption, replacing it with ultra-processed/manufactured foods is not the route to a healthy lifestyle. The onus is on you to try to exclude from your diet not just wheat, but these other Frankenfoods too, and find a different way of eating – and that can seem like a huge challenge when faced with supermarket shelves stuffed with processed products.

The solution: go back to basics

So, what's the alternative? In my recipes I use eggs, butter, olive oil and ground linseed as binding agents. These are all naturally produced, real foods and totally safe for anyone who needs to avoid wheat.

A good rule of thumb is: don't buy any food that has ingredients you can't pronounce or wouldn't exist on their own. Have a think back to what your grandparents would have eaten and stick to that principle and the first four aisles in the supermarket. That's where you'll find fresh fruit, vegetables, nuts, seeds, meat and fish. Fill up your basket there, then just go and pay! Cooking with real food is the answer.

As well as using real ingredients that are as an unprocessed as they can be (even almond flour has been processed i.e. the nuts have been ground down to flour!), my other aim is to keep the cost down as much as possible. Yes, almond flour is more expensive than wheat flour. However, due to its high protein content (24g of protein per 100g / cup - that's a whopping amount!), you need a smaller portion as it satisfies your hunger more efficiently and keeps you fuller for longer. Did you know your body also uses more calories to burn protein than to burn carbs?!

You can buy almond and chestnut flours online or from some health food stores. I haven't seen them in any of the big supermarkets in the UK. Note: almond flour is a different product to ground almonds, which are more commonly sold. If you use ground almonds instead of almond flour, your finished bake will have a very grainy texture.

Stock your larder with these frequently used ingredients: almond flour, cornflour, ground linseed, chestnut flour, baking soda/bicarbonate of soda, baking powder, sea salt, unsalted grass-fed butter (Kerrygold is one that is widely available in the UK), herbs and spices, sea salt flakes, eggs, and caster sugar.

If you have these items of kitchen equipment, they will prove invaluable:

- food blender (or a wooden spoon and a mixing bowl);
- weighing scales or US-size measuring cups;
- measuring spoons;
- spatula;
- electric whisk (or a hand-held metal balloon whisk);
- a metal or silicone 1lb (900g) loaf tin;
- cake tins;
- reusable liners to line loaf tins, cake tins and baking sheets (or baking paper/parchment. It is different to greaseproof paper as it does not require greasing);
- a lemon squeezer;
- and large and small mixing bowls.

Happy baking!

APPLE AND HONEY CAKE

I have adapted Nigella Lawson's recipe for Honey Cake with Dates and Apples by making it completely gluten free with almond flour and to showcase apple as the star of the show.

Makes 10 slices

Ingredients:
12 large rings of dried apple
100ml / $2/5$ cup freshly brewed Earl Grey tea
80g / ½ cup dates, de-stoned and chopped
350g / $2^1/_3$ cup eating apples, peeled and cored
1 large orange, zest and juice
125ml / ½ cup light olive oil
150ml / $3/5$ cup runny honey, plus an extra 2 tablespoons to glaze
100g / ½ cup dark brown sugar
2 large eggs, beaten
150g / 1½ cup almond flour
¼ teaspoon crushed sea salt
1 teaspoon raw cacao powder
100g / $7/8$ cup walnuts, chopped
1½ teaspoons bicarbonate of soda/baking soda
1½ teaspoons boiling water

Instructions:
1. Soak the apple rings in the freshly brewed tea for 5 minutes.
2. Line an 8"/20cm springform tin with baking parchment or a reusable liner.

3. Drain the apple rings and arrange them in the bottom of the tin. (The bottom of the cake will become the top, when it is turned out).
4. Cut the eating apples into ½"/1cm dice and place in a small saucepan with a lid.
5. Add the zest of the orange, 3 tablespoons of the juiced orange and 1 tablespoon of the measured olive oil.
6. Put the lid on the saucepan and cook on a low heat for 5 minutes or until the apples are tender.
7. Add the chopped dates and 1 more tablespoon of orange juice.
8. Cook, uncovered, for 4-5 minutes until you can easily mash the apples and dates with a fork.
9. Take the pan off the heat and leave it to cool for 10 minutes.
10. Set the oven to 350°F/180°C/160°C fan oven.
11. In a medium size mixing bowl, add the rest of the olive oil, honey, dark brown sugar and beaten eggs. Mix together gently until everything is just incorporated.
12. In a separate large mixing bowl, mix the almond flour, raw cacao powder, chopped walnuts and crushed sea salt.
13. Pour the olive oil mix into the saucepan with the cooled apple and mix together.
14. Using a spatula, scrape the wet ingredients into the dry ingredients and stir carefully, making sure you incorporate all the flour from the bottom of the bowl.
15. In a ramekin or cup, mix the bicarbonate of soda/baking soda with an equal amount of boiling water. Allow it to fizz up then add to the cake mixture and stir in quickly.
16. Carefully spoon the cake mixture into your prepared tin, on top of the arranged apple rings. Smooth the top so the cake is even.

17. Bake in the preheated oven for 50-60 minutes or until dark brown, firm to the touch, and a skewer comes out clean, except for a few crumbs.
18. Leave the cake to cool in the tin for 10 minutes before turning out to cool completely on a cooling rack. Leave upside down.
19. Mix 1 teaspoon of orange juice with 2 tablespoons of honey, glaze the apple rings and the top of the cake whilst it is still warm.

APPLE AND RASPBERRY CRUMBLE

A classic British pudding, adaptable for every season! I was first introduced to this combination at school and have loved it ever since. In fact, I talked about it so much, my mum even put it on the menu in her coffee shop/restaurant!

Serves 6

Ingredients:

350g / 2 $^1/_3$ cups cooking apples (Bramley)
100g / $^3/_5$ cup eating apples (Cox's or Granny Smith)
400g / 3 cups raspberries - fresh or frozen
2 tablespoons soft brown sugar
1 teaspoon cinnamon

Crumble topping:

190g / 2 cups almond flour
Pinch of crushed sea salt
60g / ¼ cup unsalted butter, cut into small pieces
60g / ¼ cup demerara sugar
100g / ¾ cup unpeeled almonds, roughly chopped

Instructions:

1. Set the oven to 400°F/200°C/180°C fan oven.
2. Put a baking sheet on a middle shelf in the oven to heat up.

3. In a medium sized bowl, mix together the soft brown sugar and the cinnamon.
4. Peel and core the apples. Cut them into thick slices, about ½" / 1.5cm.
5. Put them into the bowl with the cinnamon and sugar and toss them around until the apple slices are evenly coated.
6. Add the raspberries and mix them in gently so they don't break up too much.
7. Tip the apple and raspberry mixture into an ovenproof dish. It should come ¾ of the way up the sides of the dish.
8. To make the crumble topping, tip the almond flour into a clean mixing bowl, add the butter and rub together with your fingertips until the mixture resembles breadcrumbs.
9. Mix in the sugar, crushed sea salt and chopped almonds.
10. Pack tightly over the top of the apples and raspberries. Rake the top gently with a fork for extra crispy bits of crumble.
11. Cook on the pre-heated baking sheet in the oven for 40-45 mins or until the top is nicely browned.
12. Serve with lots of hot custard.

Hints and Tips:

The crumble topping freezes well. Tip the mixture into a freezer bag and freeze after point 9 above.

BAKED VANILLA CHEESECAKE

This cheesecake needs to firm up overnight in the fridge so be sure to make it a day before you need it!

Makes 6 slices

Base Ingredients:

30g / 1/8 cup unsalted butter
95g / 1 cups almond flour
45g / 1/3 cup icing/powdered sugar
½ teaspoon vanilla extract
1/8 teaspoon crushed sea salt

Filling Ingredients:

450g / 2 cups full-fat cream cheese, room temperature
2 large eggs
30g / ¼ cup icing/powdered sugar
½ lemon, juiced
1 teaspoon vanilla extract

Blueberry Compote Ingredients:

200g / 1 cup fresh or frozen blueberries
50g / ½ cup icing/powdered sugar
1 tablespoon of water

Instructions:

1. Grease and line a 6.5"/15cm loose-bottomed or spring-form cake tin with baking parchment.
2. Set the oven to 350°F/180°C/160°C fan oven.
3. In a medium size saucepan, melt the butter.
4. Take the pan off the heat, add the almond flour, icing/powdered sugar, vanilla extract and salt.
5. Mix together until the mixture looks like wet sand.
6. Tip the mixture into the greased tin and flatten down with the back of a metal spoon until the base is compact and even.
7. Bake in the preheated oven for 15 minutes, until slightly golden.
8. Leave to cool, in the tin, on a cooling rack for 10 minutes.

While the base is cooling, prepare the filling:

1. Place the cream cheese, eggs, icing/powdered sugar, lemon juice and vanilla extract in a food blender and blitz for a few seconds.
2. Scrape down the sides. If the mixture is not totally blended, pulse in short bursts until it is. Try not to create too many air bubbles.
3. Pour the mixture into the tin on top of the cooled base. Gently smooth the top with a spatula to disperse any air bubbles.
4. Bake in the preheated oven on the middle shelf for 40 minutes. It will still be wobbly - don't be tempted to keep on cooking it!
5. Turn the oven off and leave the cheesecake in it for 10 minutes. This reduces the possibility of the top cracking. Not guaranteed! But it does help.
6. Take the cheesecake out of the oven and leave to cool, in the tin, on a cooling rack for an hour.

7. Put the cheesecake, still in the tin, in the fridge to firm up overnight. Cover it loosely with a tea towel to allow any moisture to escape.
8. Remove it from the tin when you are ready to serve it, the next day.

Serve with a blueberry compote.

Compote Instructions: Place all the ingredients in a pan and heat gently until the mixture drops off a spoon with a little reluctance. Cool to room temperature and serve with the cheesecake.

BARA BRITH

Bara brith (which means speckled bread) is a traditional Welsh recipe and one of my favourites! This tea bread benefits from soaking the dried fruits overnight so start this bread the day before.

Makes 10-12 slices

Ingredients:

150g / 1 cup sultanas
150g / 1 cup raisins
200ml / ¾ cup freshly brewed Earl Grey tea
250g / 2¼ cups almond flour
⅛ teaspoon crushed sea salt
1¼ teaspoons baking powder
1½ teaspoons mixed spice
100g / ½ cup soft dark brown sugar
3 large eggs, beaten

Instructions:

1. Tip the dried fruits into a heat proof bowl and pour over the freshly brewed tea. Give it a good mix to make sure all the fruit is separated. Cover with a tea towel and leave to soak overnight.
2. When you are ready to make the bread, set the oven to 350°F/180°C/160°C fan oven.
3. Line a 1lb/900g loaf tin with baking parchment or a reusable liner.

4. Drain the fruit.
5. Sift the almond flour, salt, baking powder and mixed spice into a large mixing bowl.
6. Mix in the drained fruit.
7. Stir in the beaten egg.
8. Spoon the mixture into the prepared tin.
9. Bake on the middle shelf in the oven for 45-55 minutes or until risen and brown. The bread should be coming away slightly from the edges of the tin and bounce back when pressed gently.
10. Leave to cool in the tin for 5 minutes then turn onto a cooling rack to cool completely. This bread is very soft when warm but firms up nicely as it cools.

Hints and Tips:

1. If you don't like Earl Grey tea, replace it with a black tea of your choice.
2. This bread improves with keeping so you can make it 2-3 days in advance and it will keep well in an airtight tin or container.
3. You can also slice it and freeze it so you can just take out a slice or two when you feel like it!

CARROT CAKE PANCAKES

Sometimes I fancy a mid-week treat but I can't justify the time (or indulgence!) of making a WHOLE cake! That's where these pancakes come in - a quick and easy treat without compromising on taste!

Makes 10-12 pancakes

Ingredients:
100g / 1 cup almond flour
½ teaspoon baking powder
½ teaspoon bicarbonate of soda/baking soda
¼ teaspoon crushed sea salt
2 tablespoons caster sugar
2 teaspoons cinnamon
¼ teaspoon grated nutmeg
30g / ¼ cup sultanas
30g / ¼ cup pecans, chopped
160g / 1¾ cup carrots, grated
2 tablespoons coconut oil, melted
120ml / ½ cup full fat/whole milk
3 large eggs, beaten
Coconut oil for frying

Serve with:
Maple syrup and mascarpone cheese

Instructions:

1. In a large mixing bowl add the almond flour, baking powder, bicarbonate of soda, salt, sugar, cinnamon, nutmeg, sultanas and pecans. Stir until well combined.
2. Add the grated carrot, melted coconut oil, milk, and beaten eggs. Mix thoroughly.
3. Heat a large, non-stick frying pan or skillet to a low/medium heat and use a little coconut oil to grease the surface.
4. Use a pointed dessert spoon or a small ladle to pour spoonfuls of batter onto the hot pan. The pancakes should be about 3.5"/9cm across. They will expand by about 0.5"/1cm as they cook so leave room between them, so they don't run into each other!
5. Cook on the first side for a few minutes, until you see small bubbles form and then start to burst. Turn over and cook for 2 more minutes. Turn the heat down - if required - to make sure the middle cooks without the outside burning.
6. Place your cooked pancakes in a folded over tea towel on a cooling rack.
7. When you take each batch of pancakes out of the pan, brush it lightly with a little more coconut oil.
8. Serve the pancakes with a spoonful of mascarpone cheese and a generous drizzle of maple syrup. Enjoy!

Hints and Tips:

1. These pancakes freeze well. Place a layer of greaseproof paper between each one.
2. Defrost thoroughly and reheat in a pan on a low heat for 1 minute on each side or 15-20 seconds on high in the microwave.

CHERRY BAKEWELL TRAYBAKE

Cherries have a short season during the UK summer so I love to make them the star of the show and use them fresh in this recipe. If you can't get them when they are in season, this recipe works extremely well with frozen sweet cherries.

Makes 16

Ingredients:

150ml / $^3/_5$ cup light olive oil
1 large, unwaxed lemon - zest and juice
125g / $^3/_5$ cup caster sugar
225g / $2^1/_3$ cup almond flour
½ teaspoon bicarbonate of soda / baking soda
1 teaspoon baking powder
3 large eggs
150g / $^2/_3$ cup fresh, pitted cherries

Instructions:

1. Set the oven to 350°F/180°C/160°C fan oven.
2. Grease and line an 8" x 8"/20cm x 20cm cake tin.
3. Measure out the light olive oil and pour into a large mixing bowl. Add the zest from the lemon and the sugar.
4. In a separate bowl, mix together the almond flour, bicarbonate of soda/baking soda and baking powder.
5. Beat 1 egg and add it to the olive oil mixture along with $^1/_3$ of the almond mixture. Whisk until thoroughly incorporated.

6. Repeat this process with the other 2 eggs and the remaining $^2/_3$ of the almond mixture.
7. Using the largest metal spoon you have, gently fold the pitted cherries into the cake mixture being careful not to break them up.
8. Pour the cake mix into your prepared tin and bake on the middle shelf in the pre-heated oven for 45 minutes or until golden brown and a skewer comes out almost clean. Check after half an hour and cover loosely with tin foil if the cake is already golden brown.
9. While the cake is cooking, juice the lemon.
10. Pour the lemon juice over the cake as soon as you take it out of the oven, before you remove it from the tin.
11. Allow the cake to cool, in the tin, for 10 minutes before turning it out onto a cooling rack.
12. Cut into 16 squares and store in an airtight tin.

Hints and Tips:

Don't be tempted to use extra virgin olive oil in this recipe! It will give your cake a very strong peppery taste that won't be pleasant!

CHEWY GINGER COOKIES

These are soft, chewy cookies - reminiscent of ginger nuts - and perfect with a strong cup of tea. The dough needs to be chilled for 30 minutes before cooking so factor that into your prep time.

Makes 12 cookies

Ingredients:

240g / 2 ½ cups almond flour
½ teaspoon baking powder
100g / ½ cup caster sugar
½ teaspoon ground cinnamon
1 teaspoon ground ginger
¼ teaspoon mixed spice
$1/8$ teaspoon crushed sea salt
2 tablespoons coconut oil, melted
2 balls of stem ginger in syrup, chopped small
1 tablespoon syrup from the stem ginger
2 tablespoons black treacle
1 large egg, beaten
½ teaspoon vanilla extract

Instructions:

1. Put the almond flour, baking powder, sugar, cinnamon, ground ginger, mixed spice and salt in a food processor and blitz for 5 seconds to mix.

2. Add coconut oil, ginger syrup, black treacle, egg and vanilla extract. Pulse until the dough just comes together.
3. Add the chopped stem ginger and mix it in with a spoon so that it doesn't get chopped any further.
4. Transfer the dough to a bowl, cover and put in the fridge to firm up for 30 minutes.
5. Heat the oven to 350°F/180°C/160°C fan oven.
6. Line 2 baking sheets with baking parchment or reusable liners.
7. Use a tablespoon and measure out a generously heaped tablespoon of mixture for each cookie.
8. Shape into a ball and press down gently to flatten a little.
9. Leave at least 2"/5cm between each cookie as they will spread a bit during baking.
10. Bake in the preheated oven for 10-12 minutes until golden brown and slightly risen.
11. Leave to cool on the baking sheet for 5 minutes before transferring to a cooling rack to cool completely.
12. Store in an airtight tin.

Hints and Tips:

If you don't have a food processor, you can use a large mixing bowl and combine the ingredients with a large metal or wooden spoon.

CRÊPES

These are perfect for pancake day! This recipe for small crêpes - known as necci - originates from Tuscany where chestnut flour is used a lot - both in sweet and savoury dishes. The flour is made from sweet chestnuts which gives it a slightly sweet flavour without adding any sugar. This recipe couldn't be easier - you simply mix equal quantities of the flour with water to make a batter. It's also sugar free as well as gluten free!

If you're looking for inspiration for your next gluten free holiday, you could do worse than book a trip to Tuscany!

Makes 8-10 crêpes

Ingredients:
275g / 2¼ cups chestnut flour
275ml / just over 1 cup water
A little olive oil, for greasing the pan

Filling:
225g / 1 cup mascarpone cheese
½ teaspoon vanilla extract
½ teaspoon ground cinnamon
1 tablespoon chestnut honey – optional

Instructions:

1. Place a clean tea towel on a cooling rack, ready for your cooked crêpes.

2. Sift the flour into a large mixing bowl.
3. Make a well in the middle, carefully pour in 200ml / ¾ cup of the water.
4. Using a wooden spoon, or a stick blender if you have one, gradually draw in the flour from the sides until you have fully incorporated all the flour. You should have a batter consistency that coats the back of a spoon (and doesn't run off!)
5. Gradually add the rest of the water, until the batter reaches this consistency. Add more, if required.
6. Leave to rest for 1 hour.
7. If the batter thickens up after 1 hour, add a little more water until you get it back to the right consistency.
8. Heat a small crêpe pan (8"/20cm) or a flat skillet over a medium heat.
9. Brush with a little olive oil.
10. Using a ladle, spoon one ladle of batter into the hot pan, quickly swirl it around the base of the pan to distribute the batter evenly. Cook for approx. 2-3 minutes or until the top of the crêpe looks dry. Flip the crêpe over and cook for approx. 1 minute. It should be nicely browned.
11. When the crêpes are cooked on both sides, transfer to a cooling rack and fold the tea towel over them to keep the crêpes warm.
12. In a medium mixing bowl, mix together the mascarpone, vanilla extract and ground cinnamon. (Drizzle with chestnut honey, if using).
13. Place a spoonful of the mascarpone mixture in each crêpe and roll into a sausage shape to serve.

Hints and Tips:

1. If you don't like cinnamon, leave it out of the filling.

2. If you want to freeze the crêpes, interleave them with squares of greaseproof paper. Once they are defrosted, reheat briefly in a warm crêpe pan on a low heat for 30 seconds on each side.
3. If you're having this as a pudding, it's lovely with a small glass of Chestnut Liqueur served over ice. Otherwise, a splash of the liqueur added to coffee makes for a decadent holiday brunch!
4. Chestnut flour is a seasonal product. It's harvested in the autumn so - if you like it - stock up! It keeps best in the freezer.

CRUNCHY LEMON AND POPPY SEED SQUARES

Makes 10 squares

Ingredients:

200g / 2 cups almond flour
2 teaspoons baking powder
2½ tablespoons poppy seeds
¼ teaspoon crushed sea salt
110g / ½ cup unsalted butter
150g / ¾ cup caster sugar
3 large eggs, beaten
120ml / ½ cup whole milk
1 large, unwaxed lemon - zest and juice
85g / ⅓ cup caster sugar

Instructions:

1. Set the oven to 350°F/180°C/160°C fan oven.
2. Line a square 8" x 8"/20cm x 20cm glass Pyrex dish or cake tin with parchment paper or a reusable liner.
3. In a medium mixing bowl stir together the almond flour, baking powder, poppy seeds, lemon zest and salt.
4. In a separate large mixing bowl, whisk the butter with the sugar until it is pale in colour, light and fluffy.
5. Add the beaten eggs gradually, whisking between each addition.
6. Carefully whisk in the milk. Don't worry if it looks a bit curdled! It won't affect the taste.

7. Fold the almond flour mixture into the egg mixture.
8. Pour the cake mix into your prepared Pyrex dish or cake tin.
9. Cook on the middle shelf of the preheated oven for 45-50 minutes until it is golden brown and a skewer comes out clean. You may need to cover it loosely with tin foil after 30 minutes if it is already golden brown by that stage.
10. Leave the cake in the tin, on a cooling rack, for 10 minutes. Then take it out of the tin to cool completely on the cooling rack.
11. When it has cooled to room temperature, use the skewer (or a fork) to poke holes across the surface of the cake.
12. Mix together the juice from the lemon with 85g / $^1/_3$ cup of caster sugar.
13. Carefully spoon the lemon juice and sugar mixture evenly across the top of your cake, all the way to the edges. Spread it around with the back of a spoon.
14. Cut into squares.

Hints and Tips:

1. Make sure the edges of the liner in your dish are high enough to allow you to lift the cake out using the liner, rather than turning it out. It will be fragile when warm.
2. When poking the holes in the top of your cooked cake, hold the skewer against the dish and measure the depth on the skewer to ¾ of the depth of the cake. This will be the depth of the holes. If you make the holes all the way to the bottom of the cake, the delicious drizzle will just leak out!

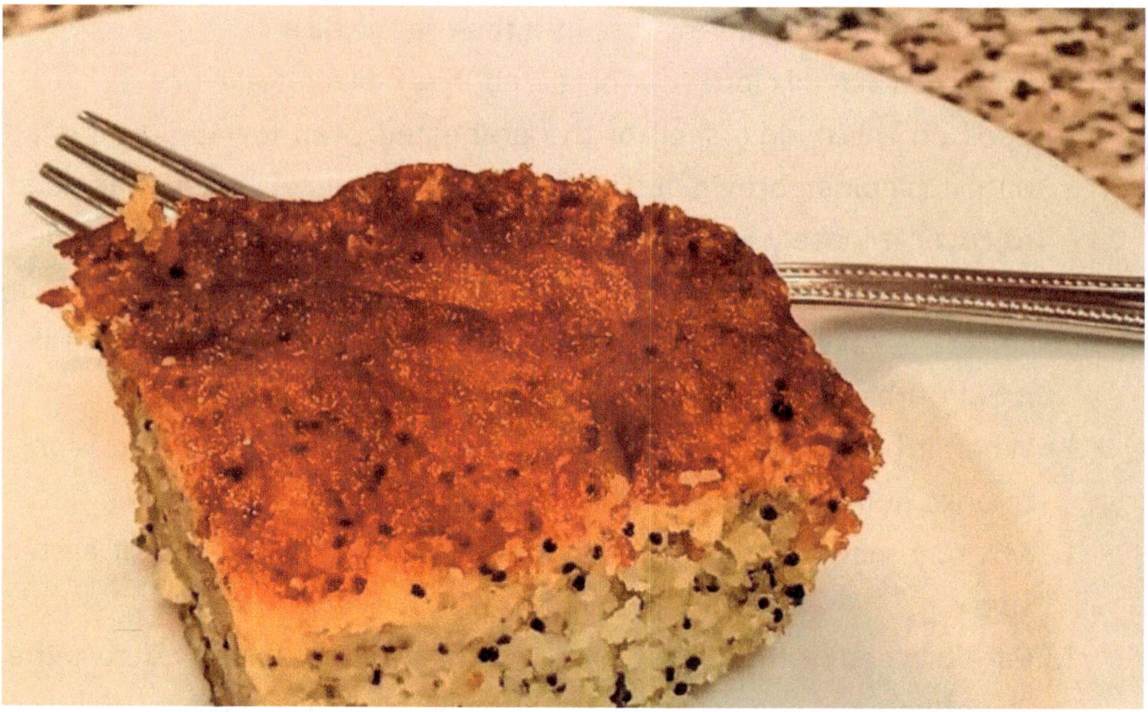

DANISH APPLE TRIFLE

For anyone who is familiar with British trifle - apart from having layers, this is nothing like it! This traditional recipe from Denmark is a delicious, layered apple pudding, with apple purée, Chantilly cream and a crunchy topping of hazelnut brittle. It looks very pretty layered in a glass serving dish or individual glass bowls.

Serves 6

Apple Purée Ingredients:
7 crisp eating apples e.g. Granny Smith
75g / $^1/_3$ cup granulated sugar
50ml / ¼ cup water
1½ teaspoons vanilla extract

Hazelnut Brittle Ingredients:
100g / ¾ cup hazelnuts
50g / ¼ cup granulated sugar

Chantilly Cream Ingredients:
450ml / $1^7/_8$ cup double/heavy cream
1 tablespoon caster sugar
¼ teaspoon vanilla extract

Instructions for Apple Purée:

1. Peel, core and cut the apples into a small dice.
2. Place a large, heavy-bottomed saucepan on a low/medium heat.
3. Add the diced apple, sugar and vanilla extract to the pan. Carefully pour over the water.
4. Leave the apples to simmer until they are soft. Stir from time to time to stop them sticking to the bottom of the pan. The apples are ready when they are tender and mash easily when pressed with the back of a spoon.
5. Set the pan aside for the apple mixture to cool.

Instructions for Hazelnut Brittle:

1. Heat the oven to 400°F/200°C/180°C fan oven.
2. Tip the hazelnuts onto a baking sheet, in a single layer, and roast in the oven for 8-10 minutes. Keep a close eye on them as they can burn very quickly. Use your nose! You will be able to smell if the nuts are burning!
3. Tip the roasted hazelnuts into a clean tea towel and give them a vigorous rub to remove all the skins.
4. Tip the sugar into a wide-bottomed pan or frying pan, turn the heat on low and wait for the sugar to melt. Once it has melted, watch for it to turn to a rich brown, caramel colour.
5. Add the skinned hazelnuts to the caramel and take it off the heat.
6. Stir the hazelnuts until they are well coated in the caramel.
7. Pour the brittle mixture onto a sheet of baking parchment or greased greaseproof paper and leave to cool.
8. When it has cooled, separate a dozen whole hazelnuts to decorate your finished pudding. Put the rest of the brittle into the food

processor and pulse until you have a fine mixture resembling breadcrumbs.

Instructions for Chantilly Cream:

1. Whip the cream to soft peak stage.
2. Tip in the sugar and add the vanilla extract.
3. Carefully mix but be careful not to overwhip the cream otherwise it will split. It will continue to thicken a little when you are assembling the pudding.

The pudding is now ready to be assembled.

1. Start with a layer of apple purée, followed by a thin layer of the blitzed hazelnut brittle, then a layer of Chantilly cream. In a large serving dish, you will probably manage 2 layers of each.
2. Finish with a layer of blitzed hazelnut brittle and scatter with the reserved, whole, caramelised hazelnuts.

Hints and Tips:

1. If you take the caramel off the heat too early, it will be overly sweet. If you leave it to get very dark brown, it will have a bitter taste. The trick is to get an in-between, light mahogany colour to it.
2. Instead of using a spoon to stir the sugar, swirl it around the bottom of the pan to distribute the caramel and get an even colour without any of it catching and burning.
3. This keeps well in the fridge for up to 24 hours so can be made well in advance. Any longer than that and the brittle will start to go soggy.

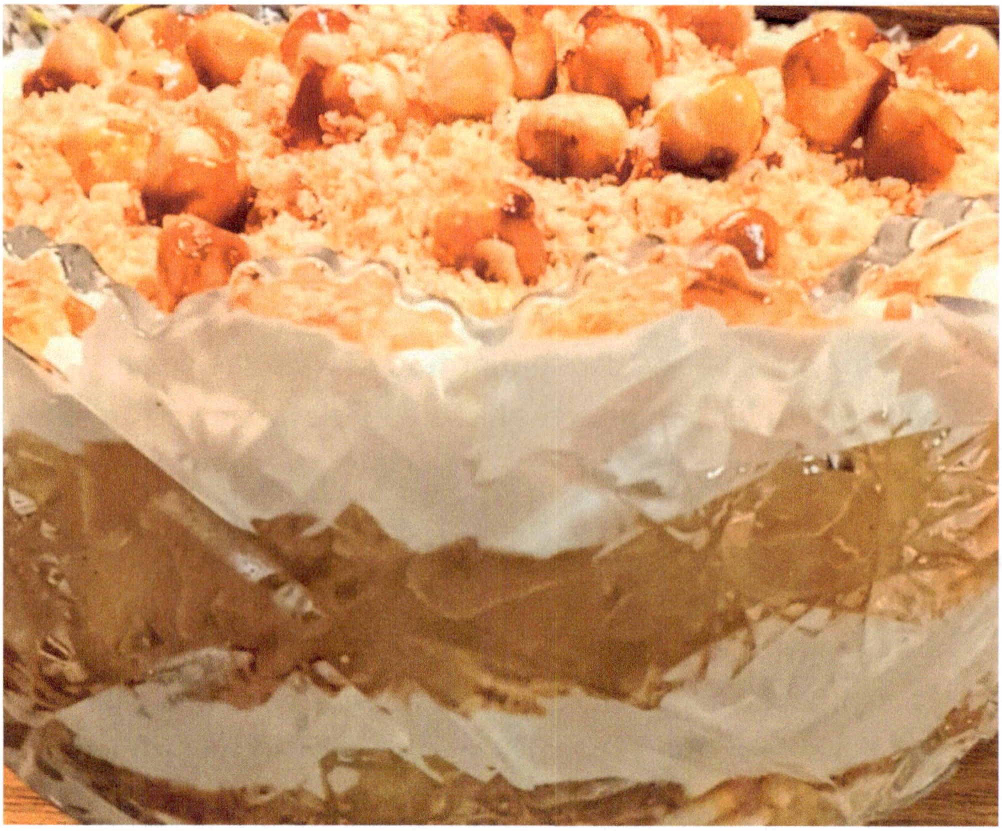

DARK CHOCOLATE TIFFIN

This is a very intense chocolate treat! It's also virtually sugar free as there's no added sugar in it and very little in the dark chocolate. The squares are small but absolutely hit the spot for a healthy chocolate fix whenever you need one! And definitely not one for the children - adults only!

Ingredients:

100g / $^3/_5$ cup dark chocolate (minimum 70% cocoa solids)
60ml / ¼ cup coconut oil, melted
60ml / ¼ cup crunchy peanut butter
¼ teaspoon crushed sea salt
$^1/_8$ teaspoon vanilla extract
¼ teaspoon ground cinnamon
¼ teaspoon ground cardamom seeds (about 3 or 4 pods)
2 teaspoons mixed seeds (a mix of sunflower, pumpkin, golden linseed, hemp and sesame - whatever you have to hand)
45g / $^1/_3$ cup hazelnuts, chopped

Instructions:

1. Line a 4" x 6"/10cm x 15cm dish with baking parchment or a reusable liner.
2. Take the seeds out of the cardamom pods and crush in a pestle and mortar until they resemble coarse breadcrumbs.

3. Break the chocolate into bite size pieces and melt in a heat proof bowl over a saucepan of simmering water on the hob or melt it in the microwave.
4. Stir in the melted coconut oil and peanut butter.
5. Stir in the salt, vanilla extract, cinnamon, crushed cardamom and mixed seeds.
6. Spoon the mixture into the prepared dish.
7. Sprinkle with the chopped hazelnuts.
8. Put in the fridge to set for 2 hours.
9. Cut into 1" / 2.5cm squares and enjoy!
10. Store in an airtight container in the fridge.

Hints and Tips:

1. The higher the chocolate content, the lower the sugar in the recipe. Dark chocolate with 85% cocoa solids works well but I don't recommend going higher than that as the end result becomes a bit too bitter.
2. If you melt the chocolate in a bowl over simmering water, rest the bowl on a tea towel, in between the bowl and the water. This stops the bowl getting too hot and the chocolate from burning. Be careful that the bowl is not touching the water either, to prevent burning.
3. If you melt the chocolate in the microwave, cook for 1 minute, stir, then cook on 20 second blasts until the majority of the chocolate has melted. Don't keep cooking until it is all completely melted as it will keep on cooking when you take it out and may split or burn. The residual heat will melt any remaining pieces of chocolate.

GRANNY'S PANCAKES

My Scottish granny made the most wonderful pancakes. She used honey that gave them a distinct flavour and tasting these takes me back to my childhood in her kitchen.

Scottish pancakes are smaller than American pancakes although about the same thickness.

Makes 8 pancakes

Ingredients:
2 large eggs
60ml / 4 tablespoons whole milk (more if needed)
1 tablespoon runny honey (or maple syrup)
1 teaspoon vanilla extract
130g / $1^{1}/_{3}$ cups almond flour
¼ teaspoon crushed sea salt
1 teaspoon baking powder
Unsalted butter or coconut oil for frying

Instructions:

1. Break the eggs into a medium sized bowl and whisk.
2. Add the milk, honey (or maple syrup) and vanilla extract.
3. Add the almond flour, salt and, finally, baking powder.

4. Give it a good stir until all the flour is incorporated into the batter.
5. If your batter is very thick, you may need to add a dash more milk. Add a teaspoon at a time so you don't make the batter too thin. The batter should fall off the spoon with a little bit of reluctancy!
6. Heat a large, non-stick frying pan or skillet over a low to medium heat. Brush the pan with butter or coconut oil and use a pointed dessert spoon to pour the batter into the pan. The pancakes should be about 8cm/3.5" in diameter. Make sure you leave sufficient room between the pancakes to turn them over.
7. Cook for approx. 3 mins on each side and turn the heat down if required to make sure the middle cooks without the outside burning.
8. Place your cooked pancakes on a cooling rack.
9. When you take each batch of pancakes out of the pan, brush the pan lightly with a little more butter or coconut oil.
10. Serve with strawberries and clotted cream, or almond butter and blueberries, or whatever other toppings you fancy! Granny spread them with butter and honey.

Hints and Tips:

1. If you want to make the recipe totally sugar free, swap the maple syrup or honey for 1 teaspoon of ground cinnamon. Although the pancakes won't be as sweet, cinnamon has a naturally sweet flavour so will help make the pancakes taste sweeter.
2. These pancakes are more delicate than regular wheat flour pancakes so don't be tempted to make them too big. Just treat yourself and have extra ones!
3. Almond flour cooks at a lower temperature than wheat flour so keep that heat quite low to avoid burning your pancakes.

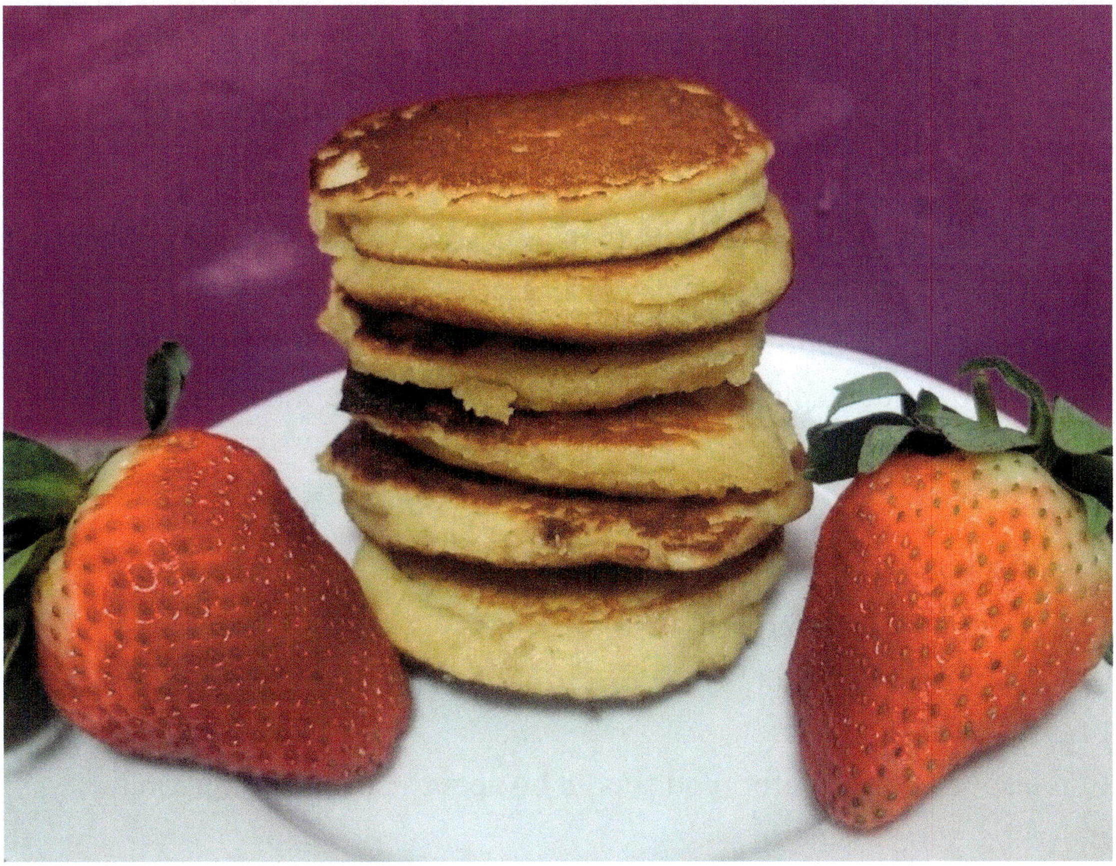

HOT CROSS BUNS

Celebrations are when I become most aware of my wheat intolerance as I miss the nostalgic associations between festivals and the traditional foods that go with them. These hot cross buns let you enjoy the delicious, spiced smells and tastes of Easter once again!

Makes 8 buns

Ingredients:
15g / 1 tablespoon dried yeast
$1/8$ teaspoon dried ginger
1 teaspoon caster sugar
1 tablespoon warm water (you should be able to put your finger in it without getting scalded)
335g / 3½ cups almond flour
55g / ¼ cup arrowroot
75g / $7/8$ cup ground flaxseed/linseed
65g / $1/3$ cup caster sugar
2 teaspoons cornflour
2 teaspoons baking powder
1 teaspoon ground cinnamon
¼ teaspoon freshly grated nutmeg
½ teaspoon mixed spice
¼ teaspoon crushed sea salt
½ orange, zest
40g / ¼ cup candied peel, chopped
40g / ¼ cup raisins

40g / ¼ cup sultanas

3 eggs, room temperature

1 tablespoon apple cider vinegar

55g / ¼ cup Greek yoghurt, room temperature

55g / ¼ cup unsalted butter, room temperature, cut into small pieces

Icing:

2 tablespoons apricot jam (without bits)

1 tablespoon juice from the orange

120g / 1 cup icing/powdered sugar, sifted

Instructions:

1. Mix the yeast with the ground ginger, 1 teaspoon caster sugar and 1 tablespoon warm water in a small bowl to activate the yeast. Set aside for 5 minutes.
2. In a large mixing bowl, mix the almond flour with the ground flaxseed/linseed, sugar, baking powder, cornflour, spices, salt, dried fruits, candied peel and orange zest.
3. Whisk the eggs in a medium mixing bowl. Whisk in the apple cider vinegar and softened butter. Whisk in the Greek yoghurt.
4. Make a well in the centre of the bowl of dry ingredients. Pour the egg mixture into the well. Add the yeast mixture.
5. Using a wooden spoon, incorporate the dry ingredients into the egg mixture, gradually pulling in the dry ingredients from the wall of the well until they are fully mixed in.
6. Line a baking sheet with baking parchment or a reusable liner.
7. Using wet hands, divide the dough and shape into 8 balls. Space them evenly on the lined baking sheet.

8. Place a dish on the bottom of your oven and fill it three quarters full with boiling water. This is going to turn your oven into a proving drawer to prove your buns which need a warm, humid environment.
9. Carefully lay a lightly oiled sheet of clingfilm over the buns and place the tray on the middle shelf. Leave the buns to double in size, approx. 1½ - 2 hours. If they haven't doubled in size, refill the dish with boiling water and leave to prove for another 30 - 60 minutes.
10. When the buns have doubled in size, remove them (and the dish of water) from the oven and heat your oven to 400°F/200°C/180°C fan oven.
11. Bake the buns for 20 minutes until they are browned and a skewer comes out clean. Check after 15 minutes and if they are already brown, cover loosely with tin foil.
12. Remove from the oven and leave to cool on the baking tray for 15 minutes before moving to a cooling rack to cool completely.
13. When the buns are cool, mix the sifted icing/powdered sugar gradually into the orange juice to make a thick icing. It should be quite stiff.
14. Brush the buns with warmed apricot jam then pipe with icing crosses.
15. Serve the buns split in half and spread with butter.

Happy Easter!

Hints and Tips:

1. The ground ginger is used to help the yeast make the buns rise. If you leave it out, your buns will not rise as much. The taste is not noticeable.
2. If the yeast doesn't activate, the yeast may be too old so try again with new yeast. Or the water may be too hot - or too cold! Hot water

kills yeast and cold water won't activate it successfully. It needs warm water to activate successfully.
3. If you are in the habit of substituting Xylitol for sugar, I recommend you opt for sugar in this recipe. Xylitol stops the growth of yeast and means your buns won't rise!
4. Instead of the little pots of dried-up mixed peel you can buy in the supermarket, I recommend you stock up on whole caps of candied peel (usually available in whole food stores. Otherwise, you can buy them from a well-known online retailer) and chop them up yourself. They really smell and taste of candied lemon and orange and are delicious!
5. If the dough is very sticky, oil your hands with light olive oil to shape the buns. Don't be tempted to use extra virgin olive oil as it will give the buns a very peppery taste!
6. If you don't have a piping bag, use a square of greaseproof/baking paper to form a cone and secure with sticky tape. Fill the cone with the icing, cut 2mm from the tip of the cone and pipe the crosses onto the hot cross buns.

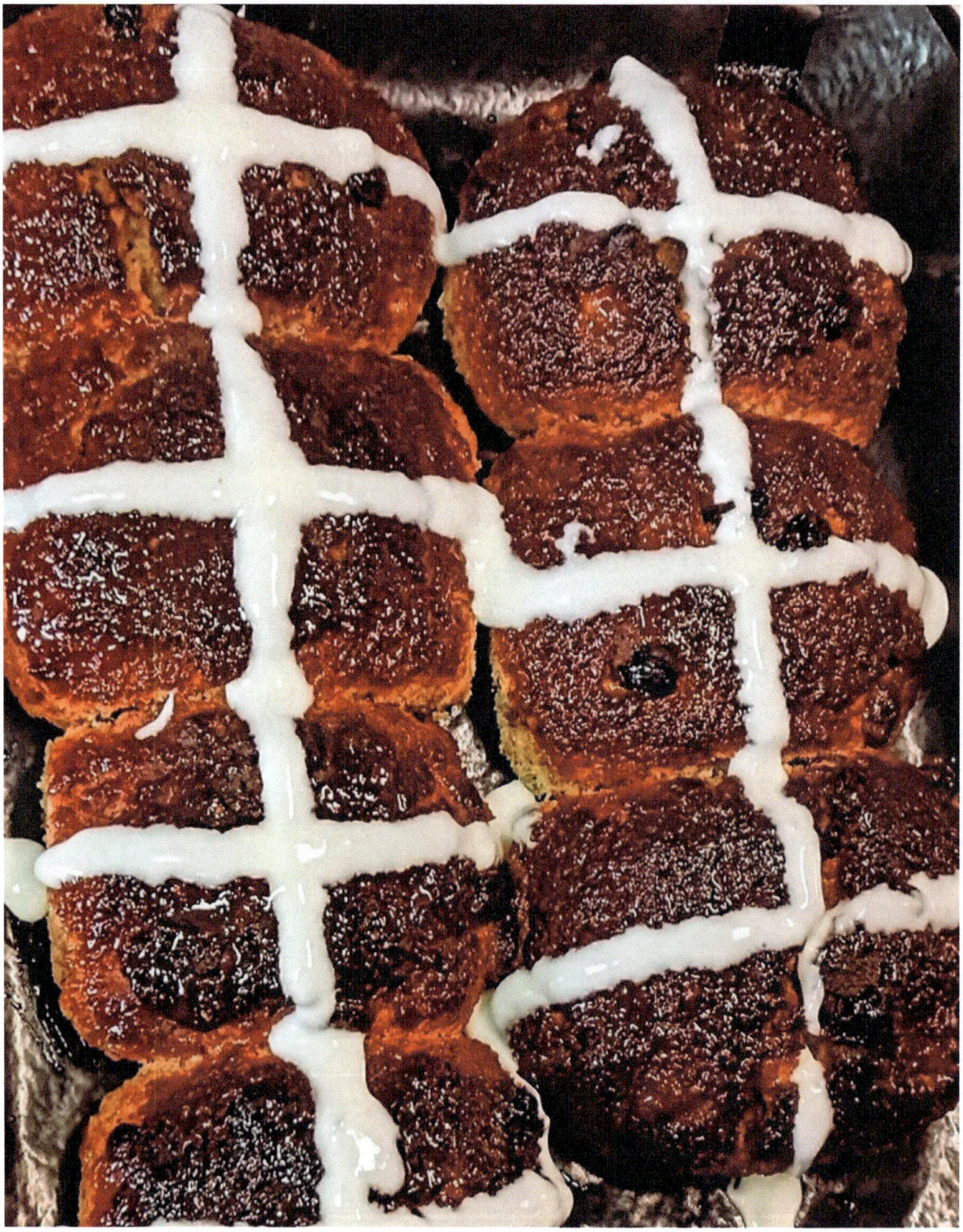

LEMON AND MARZIPAN EASTER CAKE

A gluten free twist on the traditional Simnel cake eaten at Easter. I've taken the delicious lemon flavour that runs through a Simnel cake and paired it with almond, topping it with lemon glacé icing and 11 marzipan balls that represent the remaining disciples of Jesus. Feel free to get creative and add your best Easter themed cake toppers!

Makes 12-14 slices

Cake Ingredients:
3 large unwaxed lemons
6 large eggs
225g / 1 cup caster sugar
250g / $2^3/_5$ cup almond flour
1 teaspoon baking powder
1 tablespoon apricot jam (to glaze the cooked cake before marzipanning it)

Marzipan Ingredients:
180g / 1½ cups almond flour
140g / 1 cup icing/powdered sugar
3 tablespoons water
A few drops of orange blossom water

Glacé Icing Ingredients:
100g / $^7/_8$ cup icing/powdered sugar
1 tablespoon lemon juice

Cake Instructions:

1. Heat the oven to 375°F/190°C/170°C fan oven.
2. Grease and line an 8"/21cm springform or loose-bottomed cake tin.
3. Pierce the skins of the lemons several times, put in a microwaveable dish and cover loosely with a microwaveable lid or dish. Cook on high for 3 minutes. Test with a fork. It needs to pierce the skin with ease. Cook for another minute at a time until the fork pierces the skin easily.
4. Put the whole cooked lemons in a food processor and blitz for 10 seconds.
5. Add the almond flour, sugar, baking powder and beaten eggs. Blitz until smooth.
6. Pour into the greased, lined tin and bake in the oven for one hour until a skewer comes out clean, covering with tin foil after 45 minutes if the cake is browning too much.
7. Leave in the tin to cool completely on a cooling rack before turning out to marzipan and ice.

Marzipan Instructions:

1. To make the marzipan, blitz the almond flour and the icing/powdered sugar together in a food processor for a few seconds.
2. Add the water and orange blossom water and blitz until the marzipan just forms a ball.
3. Wrap the ball of marzipan in cling film and pop in the fridge for half an hour to firm up.

To Marzipan the Cake:

1. Leave the cake turned upside down as this gives you a flat and even surface to work with.
2. Cut the marzipan in half. Using the cake tin as your guide, roll one half of the marzipan into a circle, the same size as the cake tin. Trim the edges with a sharp knife.
3. Place a saucer, upside down, in the centre of the cake.
4. Add a few drops of boiling water to the apricot jam in a small bowl to make it spread more easily and brush it over the surface of cake that is not covered by the saucer. Then remove the saucer.
5. Using a fish slice or cake lifting spatula, carefully lift the rolled marzipan circle onto the cake.
6. Place the saucer in the middle of the marzipan circle and carefully cut round it, taking care not to cut into the surface of the cake. Remove this piece of marzipan and add it to the remaining dough.
7. Make 11 equal sized balls out of the remaining marzipan.
8. Brush the marzipan circle on the cake with apricot glaze, then space the marzipan balls evenly around the edge of the cake. Keep them towards the centre as they have a tendency to roll off if they are too close to the outside edge!
9. Glaze the marzipan balls with apricot glaze.
10. Heat the grill to a low heat and put the cake under it, a couple of shelves down so that it doesn't burn.
11. Check the cake every 10 seconds as it can burn very quickly and easily. Turn if necessary so the marzipan browns evenly.
12. Once the marzipan balls are a medium brown colour, remove the cake from the oven.

Glacé Icing Instructions:

1. In a small bowl, mix the sieved icing/powdered sugar with 1 tablespoon of lemon juice. The icing should coat the back of a spoon thickly, without sliding off.
2. Carefully pour the glacé icing into the empty circle in the middle of the cake. Be careful it does not overflow!
3. Once the icing has settled (about 20-30 minutes) feel free to decorate with your cake toppers. Happy Easter!

Hints and Tips:

1. If the marzipan dough is too dry, add a few drops more water until it comes together. If it is too wet, add a tablespoon of almond flour at a time until it is drier and forms a ball.
2. **This cake is nice and moist so it keeps very well without drying out. It will see you through the whole of Easter weekend so you can be well prepared and have it ready a day early.**

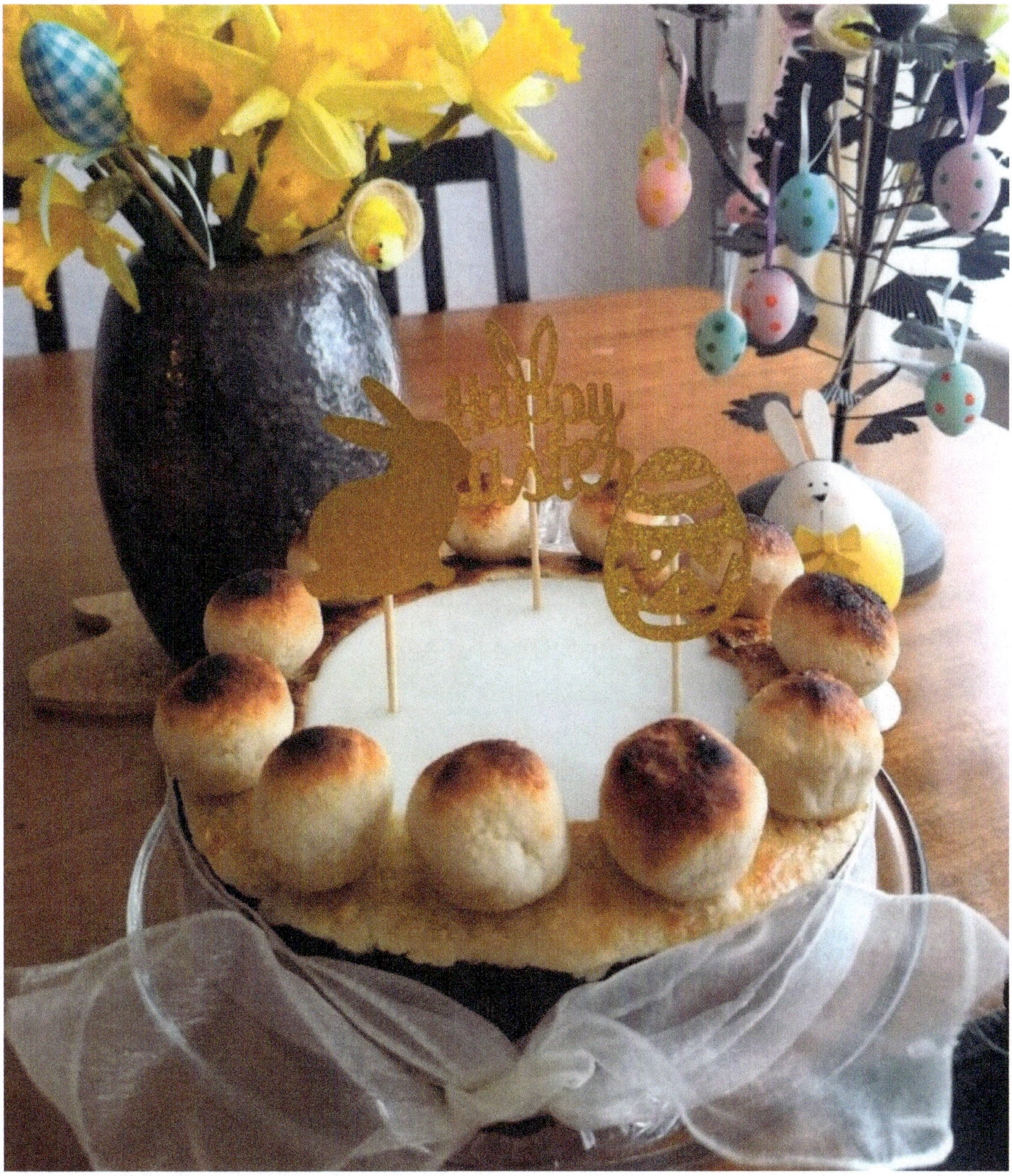
Happy

LEMONY SHORTBREAD ROUNDS

These are crispy on the outside, slightly chewy on the inside with a wonderfully fresh, lemony flavour. The dough is ready in only a few minutes, but it needs a good 1-2 hours in the fridge to firm up before slicing and baking, so I recommend you plan to make it well in advance of wanting to enjoy them!

Makes 16

Ingredients:
75g / ⅓ cup room temperature, unsalted butter
100g / ½ cup sugar
240g / 2 ½ cups almond flour
¼ teaspoon crushed sea salt
1 lemon - zest of the whole lemon, and juice of ½ the lemon
1 tablespoon caster sugar, for sprinkling (optional)

Instructions:

1. In a mixing bowl, beat the butter and sugar together until they are light in colour and fluffy.
2. Add the almond flour, salt and lemon zest and beat again until the mixture looks like wet sand.
3. Add the lemon juice gradually until the dough comes together. Press with your fingers to check. The dough will be very soft.
4. Grease a length of cling film with a little butter, place the dough on it and shape into a log about 2"/5cm in diameter.

5. Wrap it tightly in the clingfilm, in a sausage shape. Smooth each end.
6. Place in the fridge for at least 1 hour or until very firm. If required, give it another little roll after 30 minutes once it's had a chance to firm up a little, to make sure the dough is round.
7. Line a baking sheet with baking parchment or a reusable liner.
8. Use a sharp knife to cut the dough into 16 rounds and place on the lined baking sheet. The shortbread will spread a little during baking so leave space around them.
9. Use the prongs of the fork and gently press round the edges of each shortbread, to make a pattern of approx. 1cm all the way round.
10. Use the fork to prick the centre of each shortbread 3 times.
11. Put the baking sheets with the shortbread on them back in the fridge for 5 minutes to firm up before baking.
12. Set the oven to 350°F/180°C/160°C fan oven.
13. Cook for 12-15 minutes or until the shortbread is lightly golden in colour. They should still be quite pale.
14. If you like your shortbread slightly sweeter, sprinkle with a light dusting of caster sugar as soon as they come out of the oven.
15. Allow to cool on the baking sheet for 10 minutes before moving to a cooling rack to cool completely.
16. Store in an airtight tin.

Hints and Tips:

1. If the dough isn't coming together, add a little more lemon juice.
2. If it becomes too wet, add an extra teaspoon of almond flour, mixing between each addition, until it is less wet.
3. The coldest place in your fridge is the back of the bottom shelf so, if you want your dough to firm up as quickly as possible, that's the place to put it!

4. This dough freezes well. Shape it into a sausage as above, and place in a freezer bag. Defrost in the fridge for approx. 6 hours (or the day before you need it), ready for slicing and baking.

PEAR AND FRANGIPANE TART

This tart is a proper show-stopper! If you want to wow friends and family for a special occasion, make this for them!

Serves 8-10

Pastry Case Ingredients:
240g / 2½ cups almond flour
50g / ¼ cup caster sugar
¼ teaspoon crushed sea salt
55g / ¼ cup unsalted butter
½ teaspoon vanilla extract
1 large egg, beaten

Filling Ingredients:
250g / 1 cup unsalted butter
250g / 1¼ cups caster sugar
250g / 2½ cups ground almonds
4 large eggs, beaten
4 large pears, (fresh or canned) peeled, cored, and sliced in half (top to bottom)
1 tablespoon icing/powdered sugar - to decorate
20g flaked almonds, toasted

Instructions:

Start by making the pastry case.

1. Grease a 10"/25cm tart tin or a metal flan ring, placed on a lined baking sheet.
2. Preheat the oven to 400°F/200°C/180°C fan oven.
3. Melt the butter.
4. Put all the ingredients for the pastry case into a food processor and pulse until the pastry just comes together. You don't want to overwork the almond flour otherwise it will turn into almond butter!
5. Press the pastry into the flan ring making sure you get it into all the edges and corners and smooth with the back of a metal spoon to make sure it is even.
6. Using a fork, pierce holes evenly across the base of the pastry case. This stops it puffing up during cooking.
7. Bake on the top shelf of the preheated oven for 10 minutes or until slightly golden and the base of the pastry case isn't greasy to the touch. Check after 7 minutes. If necessary, carefully place some tin foil around the edges of the pastry case to stop it browning too much.
8. When the case is cooked, reduce the oven temperature to 325°F/160°C/140°C fan oven.

While the pastry case is cooking, prepare the frangipane filling.

1. Using an electric whisk, cream the butter and sugar together in a large bowl until they are very pale in colour and doubled in size.
2. Mix in one quarter of the ground almonds.
3. Add the eggs gradually and beat well between each addition to make sure they are fully incorporated.

4. Mix in the remaining three quarters of ground almonds.
5. Spoon the frangipane filling into the cooked pastry case and spread out evenly.
6. Arrange the pears in a circle - like the spokes of a wheel - in the frangipane, round side up, and press gently into the frangipane so that the pears are at an even height with the almond mixture.
7. Protect the pastry edges of the tart with some thin strips of tin foil.
8. Bake the tart in the oven, at the reduced heat, for 50-60 minutes. It should be golden brown and slightly risen.
9. When you have taken the tart out of the oven, switch to grill and toast the flaked almonds for a couple of minutes. Keep a close eye on them so that they don't burn. Use your nose!
10. Using a small sieve, dust the tart with icing/powdered sugar and sprinkle with the toasted almonds.

Hints and Tips:

This pastry doesn't roll in the same way that pastry made with wheat flour does, because it doesn't have gluten in it. Using the back of a metal spoon to flatten it out directly in the flan ring works very effectively!

Best served warm with pouring cream or ice cream.

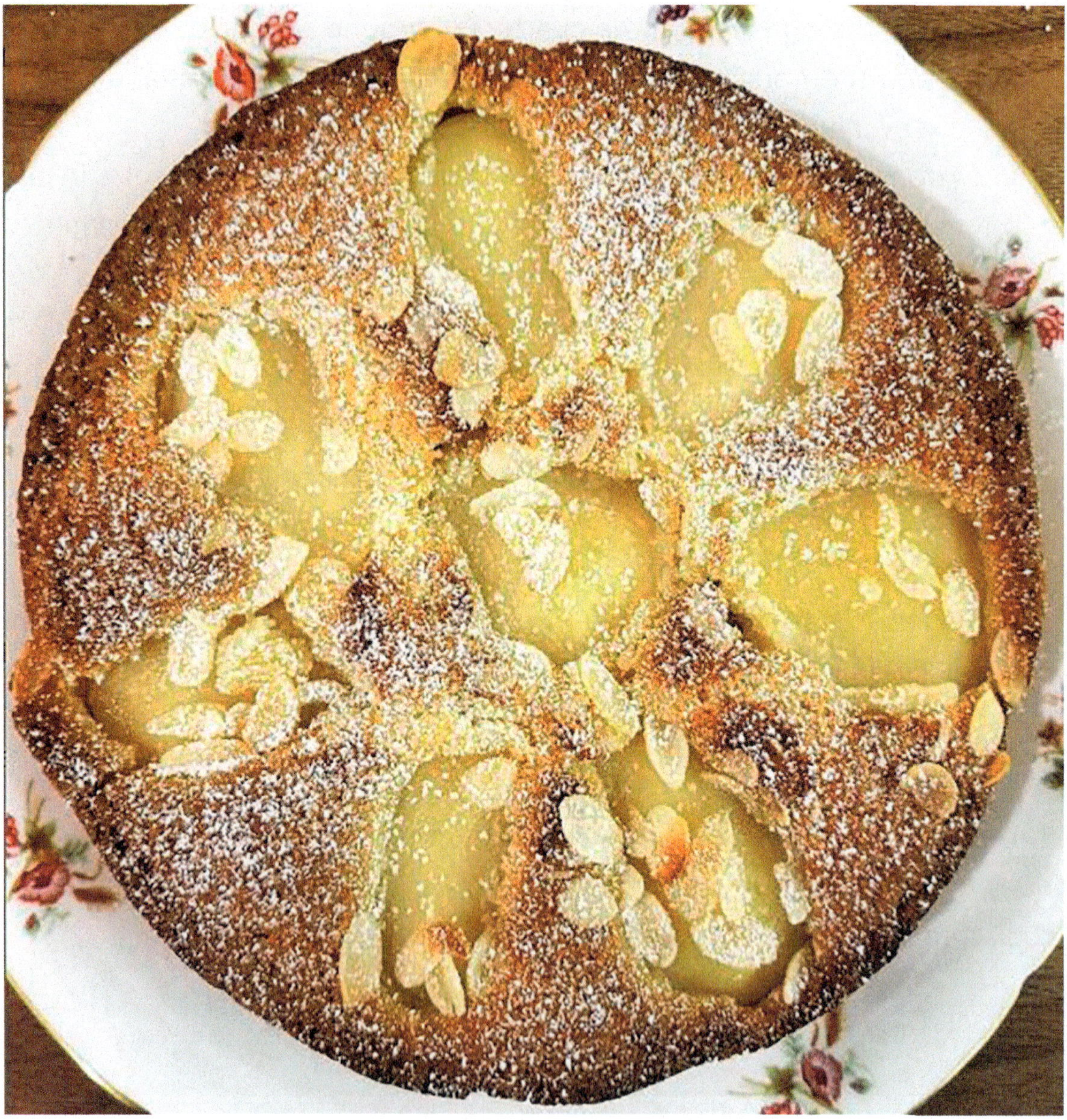

SCONES

Cream teas immediately remind me of sunny summer holidays in Cornwall. Sitting by the sparkling sea, a scone piled ludicrously high with jam and Cornish clotted cream, washed down with lots of fragrant Earl Grey tea.

The Cornish way is jam followed by cream whereas the Devon way is cream followed by jam. How do you eat yours?!

Makes 6 scones

Ingredients:

215g / 2¼ cups almond flour
45g / ¼ cup caster sugar
1½ teaspoon baking powder
50g / ¼ cup unsalted butter, melted
1 large egg, beaten

To serve:

Strawberry jam
Clotted cream

Instructions:

1. Preheat the oven to 350°F/180°C/160°C fan oven.
2. Line a baking sheet with baking parchment or a reusable liner.

3. Mix the almond flour, caster sugar and baking powder together thoroughly.
4. In a separate, small bowl whisk together the melted butter with the beaten egg.
5. Make a well in the centre of the almond flour mix and tip in the butter and egg mixture.
6. With a large metal spoon, gradually draw in the almond flour mix to the egg mix until well incorporated.
7. Using your hands, shape the dough into 6 scones. Make them about 1.5"/3.5cm across and leave them quite high as they will spread in the oven.
8. Space them apart by 2"/5cm on the baking sheet.
9. Bake on a middle shelf for 20-23 minutes until risen and golden brown.
10. Carefully remove them from the baking tray to a cooling rack to cool completely.
11. Best enjoyed cut in half, spread with strawberry jam and clotted cream and served with a cup of tea.

Hints and Tips:

1. The dough should be quite stiff. If it's a bit too wet to shape the scones so that they hold their shape, add ½ a tablespoon of extra almond flour at a time until the scones hold their shape.
2. The scones are quite fragile when warm but will firm up as they cool down so that you can slice them easily and they won't crumble.
3. They freeze well. Defrost at room temperature.

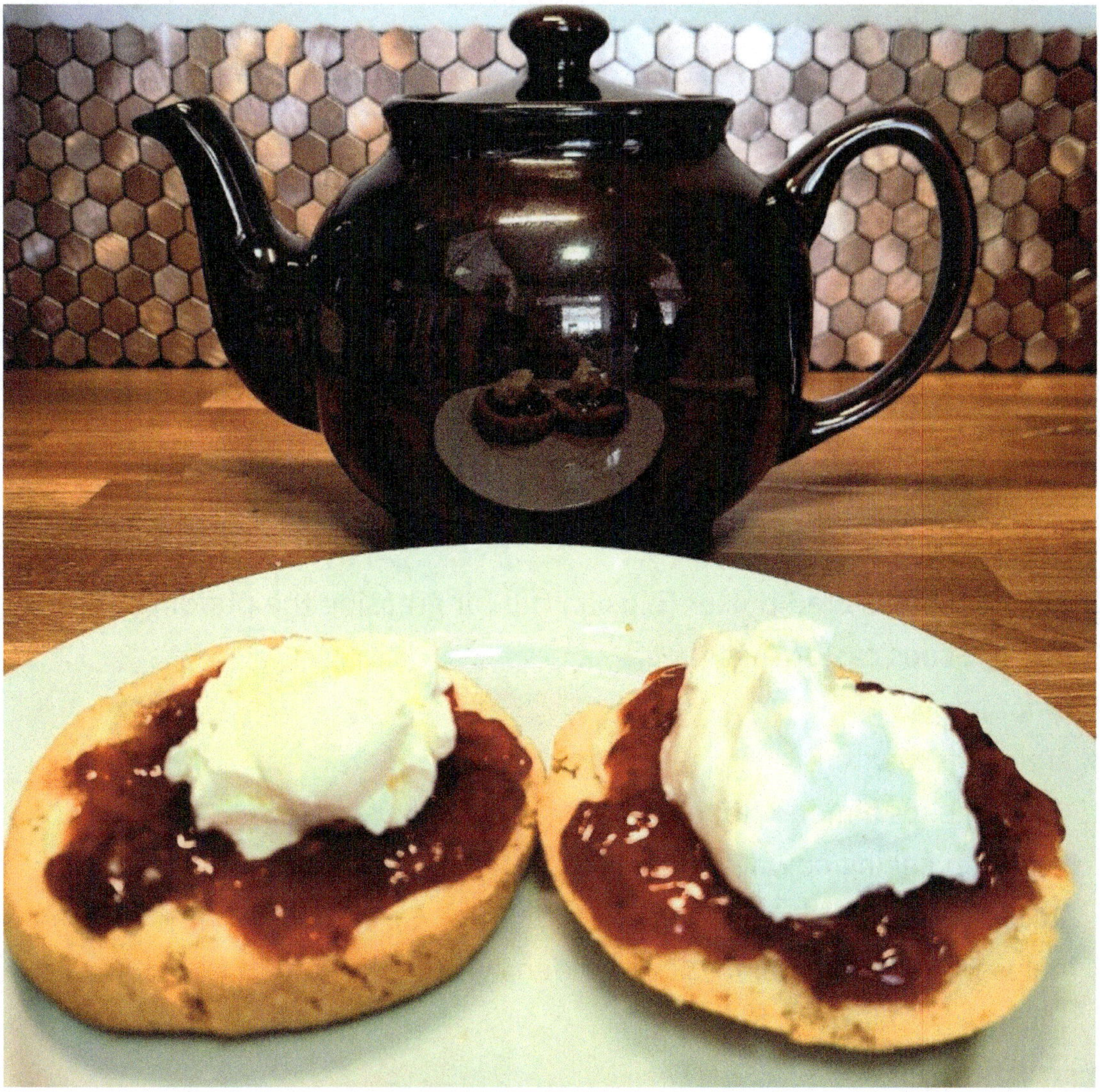

STEAMED TREACLE SPONGE PUDDING

This pudding embodies the absolute pleasure of cooking and celebrates slow food. Celebrate the weekend and treat yourself to this after a delicious Sunday roast.

Serves 6-8

Ingredients:

175g / ¾ cup unsalted butter (plus a little for greasing the pudding basin)
175g / 1½ cups caster sugar
1 lemon, zest
3 large eggs, beaten
150g / 1¾ cups almond flour
1 teaspoon baking powder
$1/8$ teaspoon crushed sea salt
2 tablespoons milk 80ml / $1/3$ cup golden syrup

Instructions:

1. Lightly grease a 2 pint / 1.1 litre pudding basin. Cut a small circle of baking parchment and use it to line the base of the pudding basin.
2. In a large mixing bowl, cream the butter and sugar together until they are pale in colour. Add the beaten eggs very gradually and continue to whisk between additions.
3. Carefully whisk in the milk.
4. Now add the lemon zest, almond flour, baking powder and salt and gently fold into the mixture with the largest metal spoon you have.

5. Pour the golden syrup into the pudding basin.
6. Carefully spoon in the sponge mixture on top of the syrup.
7. Cover the pudding basin with a layer of baking parchment and tin foil, secure tightly round the rim with string and place in a pan of simmering water to steam for 2 hours. The water should come ¾ of the way up the pudding basin. Top up as required so that the pan doesn't boil dry.
8. Leave to stand for 10 minutes before turning out.
9. Serve with lashings of hot vanilla custard!

Hints and Tips:

1. Make sure that the layer of baking parchment and tin foil is not in contact with the boiling water otherwise it will soak up water and make the pudding soggy.
2. It helps to have someone else on hand to use their finger to place on the string when tying the knot. It helps make sure the string doesn't slip and will give a really tight knot.
3. If you have a reusable plastic pudding basin, use the lid that comes with it.
4. Instead of cooking the sponge on the hob, you can use a slow cooker, with the lid on, with the setting set on high. It will take 3 hours instead of 2 to steam the pudding. The benefit is that you won't need to top the water up or adjust the heat.

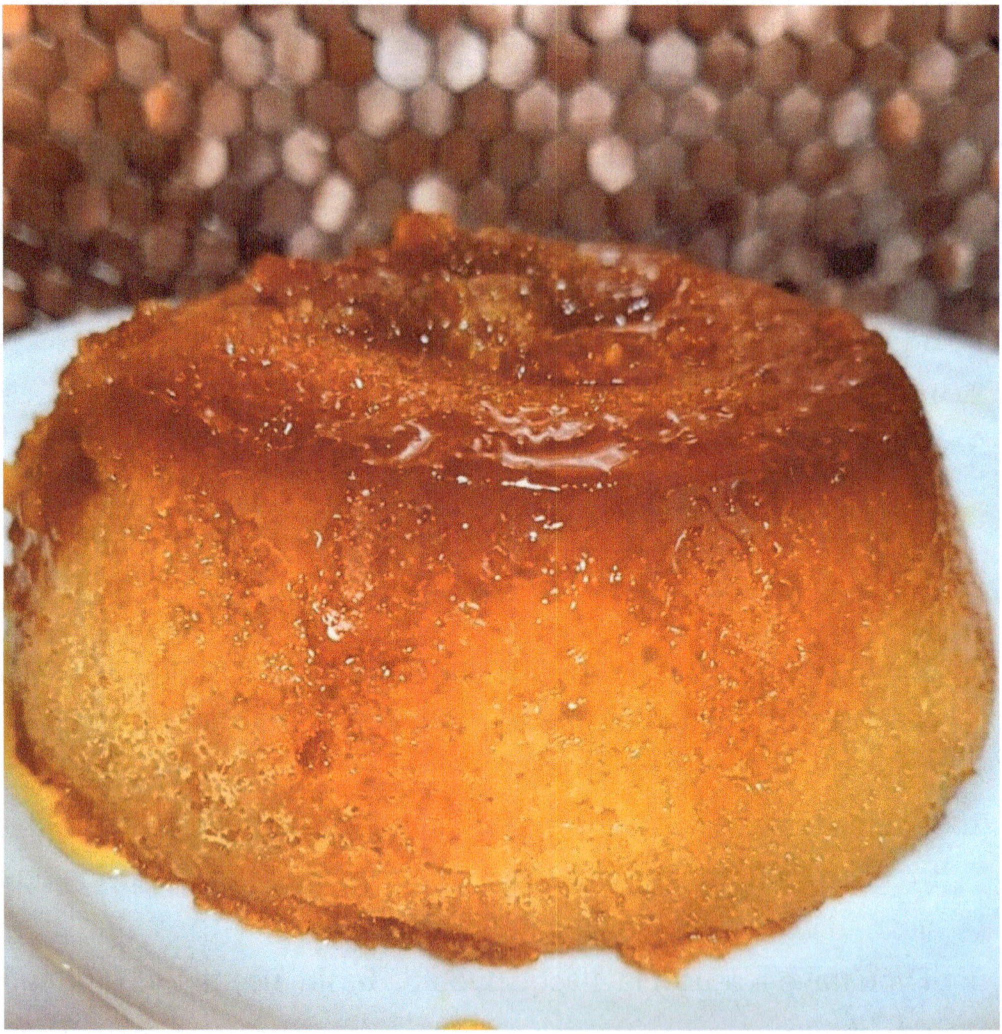

STICKY TOFFEE PUDDING

This all-time classic is made up of a fluffy yet moist date sponge with a warm toffee sauce poured over it. Although there are various claims about who invented it, there's no doubt its popularity came about in the 1970s thanks to Francis Coulson and Robert Lee of the Sharrow Bay Country House Hotel in Cumbria and remains a firm favourite - to this day - the world over. I have tried to stick (no pun intended) as closely as I can to their recipe, as an homage to them.

Makes 8 portions

Cake Ingredients:
225g / $1^{1}/_{3}$ cups dates
290ml / 1¼ cup freshly brewed English Breakfast tea
110g / ½ cup unsalted butter, room temperature
110g / ½ cup caster sugar
3 large eggs, beaten
225g / $2^{1}/_{3}$ cups almond flour
1 teaspoon baking powder
1 teaspoon vanilla extract
1 tablespoon freshly brewed coffee

Toffee Sauce Ingredients:
220g / 1 cup unsalted butter
110g / ½ cup dark soft brown sugar
150ml / a generous ½ cup of double/heavy cream
$1/_{8}$ teaspoon crushed sea salt – optional

Instructions:

1. Set the oven to 350°F/180°C/160°C fan oven.
2. Chop the dates and soak them in the freshly brewed tea for 30 minutes.
3. Grease and line an 8.5"/21cm springform or loose bottomed cake tin.
4. Cream the butter and sugar together until they are very pale in colour.
5. Add the beaten eggs very gradually and continue to whisk between additions.
6. Drain the dates. Add to the mixture.
7. Mix in the vanilla essence, baking powder and the coffee.
8. Finally, fold in the almond flour.
9. Pile the cake mixture into the prepared tin and bake for 1-1.5 hours until well-browned. It will bounce back when pressed gently and a skewer will come out clean. If it needs more than 1 hour, cover loosely with tin foil to stop it browning any further.
10. Leave to cool in the tin for 10 minutes. Carefully release it from the tin, leaving the cake resting on the base of the tin and place on a cooling rack to cool completely.

While the cake is cooling, make the sauce.

1. Place all the sauce ingredients in a medium size pan, place on a low heat, stirring gently until they have all melted.
2. Now bring to the boil to allow the sauce to thicken slightly. It should just coat the back of a spoon.
3. Cut the cake into 8 slices. Serve with warm toffee sauce and vanilla ice-cream.

Hints and Tips:

1. If you don't like English Breakfast tea, you can use another black tea of your choice.
2. The salt in the toffee sauce gives it a slightly salted caramel flavour. If you're not a fan of salted caramel, leave the salt out.

SQUIDGY CHOCOLATE BROWNIES

Makes 12 brownies

Ingredients:

110g / ½ cup unsalted butter

310g / 1¾ cups 70% dark chocolate, broken into small pieces

150g / ¾ cup caster sugar

3 large eggs, beaten

1 teaspoon vanilla extract

100g / 1 cup almond flour

3 tablespoons raw cacao powder

½ teaspoon baking powder

¼ teaspoon crushed sea salt

Instructions:

1. Set the oven to 400°F/200°C/180°C fan oven.
2. Grease and line an 8" x 8"/20cm x 20cm baking tin, leaving some overhang to help you lift the brownies out after they are cooked.
3. Melt the butter and 225g/1 cup of the chocolate in a heat proof bowl over a saucepan of simmering water on the hob or melt it in the microwave. Stir carefully to make sure they are properly mixed together. Set aside to cool a little.
4. In a large mixing bowl, mix together the almond flour, raw cacao powder, baking powder and crushed sea salt.
5. Once cooled, pour the chocolate into a mixing bowl, add the sugar and beat to bring together.
6. Add the vanilla extract to the beaten eggs.

7. Very gradually add the eggs to the chocolate mixture and continue to whisk between additions.
8. Add the dry ingredients you mixed together in step 4 along with the remaining chocolate pieces and fold in carefully.
9. Pour into the prepared tin and bake for 25 minutes or until a skewer comes out with just a little bit of brownie mixture on it.
10. Leave in the baking tin to cool completely on a cooling rack before lifting out and cutting into 12 squares.

Hints and Tips:

1. If you bake the brownies until the skewer comes out clean, your brownies will be dry instead of squidgy! On the other hand, if the skewer comes out with a lot of wet brownie mixture still on it, your brownies have not cooked enough and will just fall apart. Give them an extra 5 minutes in the oven and test again.
2. If you melt the chocolate and butter in a bowl over simmering water, rest the bowl on a tea towel, in between the bowl and the water. This stops the bowl getting too hot and the chocolate from burning. Be careful that the bowl is not touching the water either, to prevent burning.
3. If you melt the chocolate and butter in the microwave, cook for 1 minute, stir, then cook on 20 second blasts until the majority of the chocolate has melted. Don't keep cooking until it is all completely melted as it will keep on cooking when you take it out and may split or burn. The residual heat will melt any remaining pieces of chocolate.

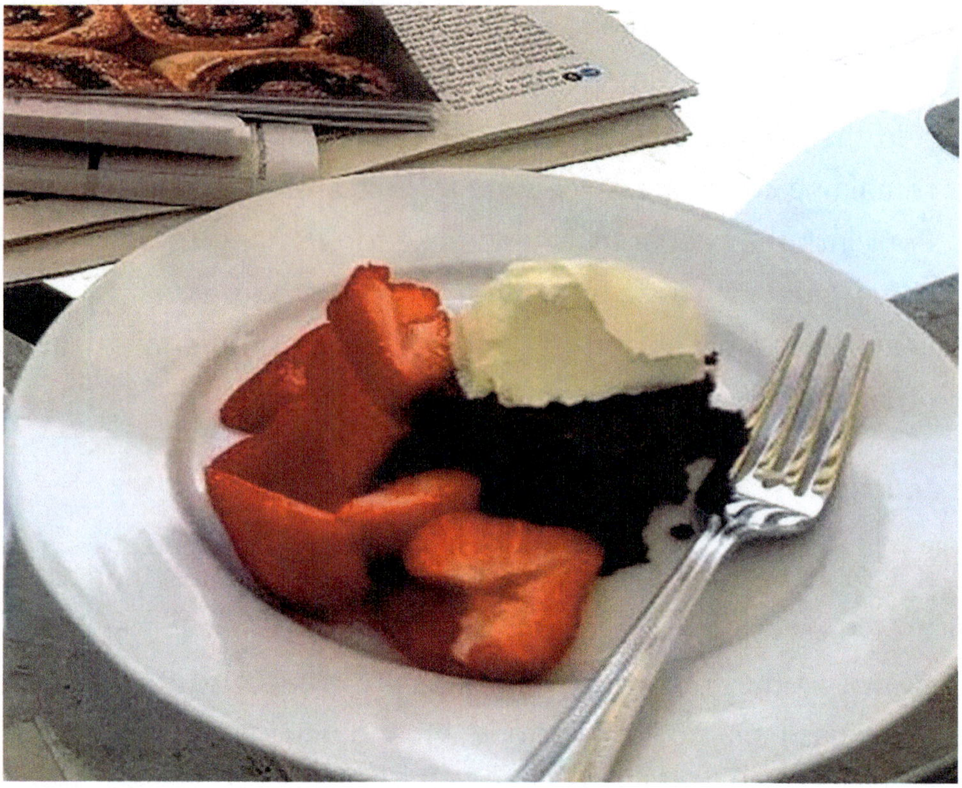

ACKNOWLEDGMENTS

I would like to thank my lovely husband, Dan, for his unfaltering faith in my abilities and his unwavering encouragement to nudge me to follow my dreams. Without him, I doubt I would have believed enough in myself for this recipe book to have materialised!

He also just so happens to be a journalist and editor by trade so I - and you! - have benefited from his skills in making this book as professional as possible! He has a finely tuned sense of taste and has frequently been requested to 'taste this' and to tell me 'what do you think of that?' and his feedback has been invaluable. Thank you, Dan.

My parents have had no small - indirect - contribution to this book by sending me to Prue Leith's school to train as a chef, straight after I left school, and led to me developing a deep-seated passion for food and cooking. Thank you.

To the many cooks and chefs out there that have inspired me, both past and present. There are too many to list them all but some of my favourites are Prue Leith (obviously!), Nigella Lawson, Delia Smith, Rose Gray and Ruth Rogers. As well as the inimitable Fanny Cradock - the original female celebrity chef - who has inspired so many others.

My final thanks go to you, dear reader, for picking up this cookery book and enjoying the recipes in it. Keep a look out for more books in the 'Nuts About' series - both sweet and savoury as well as seasonal editions and, my favourite celebration - Christmas!

ABOUT THE AUTHOR

Victoria Searle-Thomson trained at the prestigious Prue Leith's School of Food and Wine and has worked as a professional chef in the kitchens of the UK and France.

She discovered her passion for creating recipes when, at the age of ten, she had her first recipe published in a children's comic.

With an English honours degree from Oxford Brookes University, her other loves include reading and writing.

She lives by the sea in Worthing, UK, with her husband and Harris the cat.

Printed in Great Britain
by Amazon